CHOPIN
19 OF HIS MOST POPULAR PIANO SELECTIONS
A PRACTICAL PERFORMING EDITION

Portrait by Eugene Delacroix

Contents
Selections are placed in approximate order of difficulty.

ETUDE IN E MAJOR, Op. 10, No. 3	60
FANTASIE-IMPROMPTU, Op. 66 (Posthumous)	52
LARGO IN E♭ MAJOR (Posthumous)	43
MAZURKA IN A MINOR, Op. 7, No. 2	7
MAZURKA IN B♭ MAJOR, Op. 7, No. 1	4
MAZURKA IN C MAJOR, Op. 7, No. 5	10
MAZURKA IN G MINOR, Op. 67, No. 2 (Posthumous)	11
NOCTURNE IN E♭ MAJOR, Op. 9, No. 2	44
POLONAISE IN A MAJOR, Op. 40, No. 1	48
PRELUDE IN A MAJOR, Op. 28, No. 7	35
PRELUDE IN B MINOR, Op. 28, No. 6	34
PRELUDE IN C MAJOR, Op. 28, No. 1	32
PRELUDE IN C MINOR, Op. 28, No. 20	42
PRELUDE IN D♭ MAJOR, Op. 28, No. 15	38
PRELUDE IN E MINOR, Op. 28, No. 4	36
WALTZ IN A MINOR, Op. 34, No. 2	18
WALTZ IN C♯ MINOR, Op. 64, No. 2	28
WALTZ IN D♭ MAJOR, Op. 64, No. 1	24
WALTZ IN E MINOR (Posthumous)	13

Copyright © MCMXCV by Alfred Publishing Co., Inc.
All rights reserved. Printed in USA.

Book Alone
ISBN-10: 0-7390-1063-8
ISBN-13: 978-0-7390-1063-1

Book & CD
ISBN-10: 0-7390-4752-3
ISBN-13: 978-0-7390-4752-1

Cover art: A portrait of Frédéric Chopin
by A. Scheffer (1795–1858)
Courtesy of Art Resource, New York

FREDERIC CHOPIN

Drawing by Elise Radziwill

Drawing by Luigi Calamatta in 1840

Oil portrait by Ary Scheffer in 1847

In the autumn of 1829 a new figure appeared on the concert scene in Vienna. He was just 19 years old, and his name was Frederic Francois Chopin. He had graduated from the Conservatory in Warsaw and, through his teacher, Josef Elsner, and through contacts made by his father, he was introduced to a number of influential people including the music publisher, Tobias Hasslinger, and the owner of the Kärntnertor Theater who arranged for Chopin an opportunity to make his debut in his own auditorium, which was the largest in the city.

Chopin's performance was a sensation. He played his difficult *Variations on "La ci darem la mano,"* on the famous theme from Mozart's opera, *Don Giovanni.* He made free improvisations on another theme submitted by the audience. He played an improvisation on a popular melody from Boieldieu's opera *La Dame blanche.* Then he ended his program with variations on a Polish drinking song. He finished to thundering applause. Robert Schumann wrote his famous pronouncement, "Hats off, gentlemen — a genius!" He wrote even further, "No matter how little Chopin needs to be reminded of his genius, I nevertheless bow my head before such genius, such mastery, and such endeavor!"

Schumann continued to find greatness in Chopin's compositions and performances throughout his life, and each new work was greeted with great enthusiasm. "Chopin no longer writes anything that we could find in others," wrote Schumann. "He is true to himself, and with good reason."

During Chopin's lifetime, the musical scene in Europe was dominated by musicians who made their fortunes from showmanship, dazzling feats of virtuosity, fortissimo playing, and the more shallow elements of musical performance. Chopin's delicate constitution would not allow him to compete with other musical artists on these terms, and his artistic nature rebelled against it. He won his fame through the merits of his compositions, which were so full of originality and so daringly different that many of his critics found the more serious ones almost impossible to comprehend. Chopin made few public appearances, but those who heard him praised his delicate pianissimo and his complete control of nuance of dynamics. His concerts were mostly in small salons rather than in concert halls, and he always preferred to use an upright piano rather than a large grand.

During his lifetime, Chopin composed over 200 works for piano, in large and small forms. Most of these have endured and are still a part of the active repertoire of artists the world over. When he was still alive, the immense popularity of some of the smaller compositions, such as the *Mazurka* (Opus 7, No. 1), the *Waltz in Db Major* (Opus 64, No. 1), the *Nocturne in Eb* (Opus 9, No. 2) and the *Polonaise in A Major* (Opus 40, No. 1) brought him great fame, and few musicales were complete without the performance of several of these. Although Chopin wrote larger works that crowned his achievements as a composer (the *Ballades, Scherzi, Concerti,* larger *Etudes,* etc.), none bear the stamp of genius more strongly than some of his smaller works (for example, the *Preludes*).

Although Chopin did not in his lifetime enjoy fame equal to that of Mendelssohn, Liszt, or even Kalkbrenner and Hummel, today his piano works are performed more frequently than those of any of his contemporaries. He was the greatest of the romanticists (though he detested the word) and the first modernist. His innovations in pedaling and fingering, along with his introduction of new elements of style in playing, were to raise the art of piano playing to a new pinnacle.

All of Chopin's great works were completed in a life-span of only 39 years. He died October 17, 1849. In this book you will find most of the works that have enjoyed the greatest popularity over the years and are known to the majority of music lovers, including the "Raindrop" *Prelude,* the "Military" *Polonaise,* the beloved *Nocture in Eb,* and the *Etude in E Major,* Chopin's own favorite melody. Also included are the *Minute Waltz,* and the most popular of all the Mazurkas, Op. 7, No. 1, and many, many more. These are presented in accurate, carefully edited versions, which should bring you many hours of enjoyment.

The *Mazurka* is one of the traditional national dances of Poland. It always has three beats in a measure, and there is a certain accentuation of the second beat that is a characteristic of its correct performance. Musical phrases usually end on the second beat of the measure. Chopin wrote over fifty mazurkas for the piano, bringing many refinements to the style, and combining some of the rhythmic characteristics of a closely related Polish dance, the *Kouiaviak*.

MAZURKA IN B♭ MAJOR

à Monsieur Johns de la Nouvelle-Orléans

Op. 7, No. 1

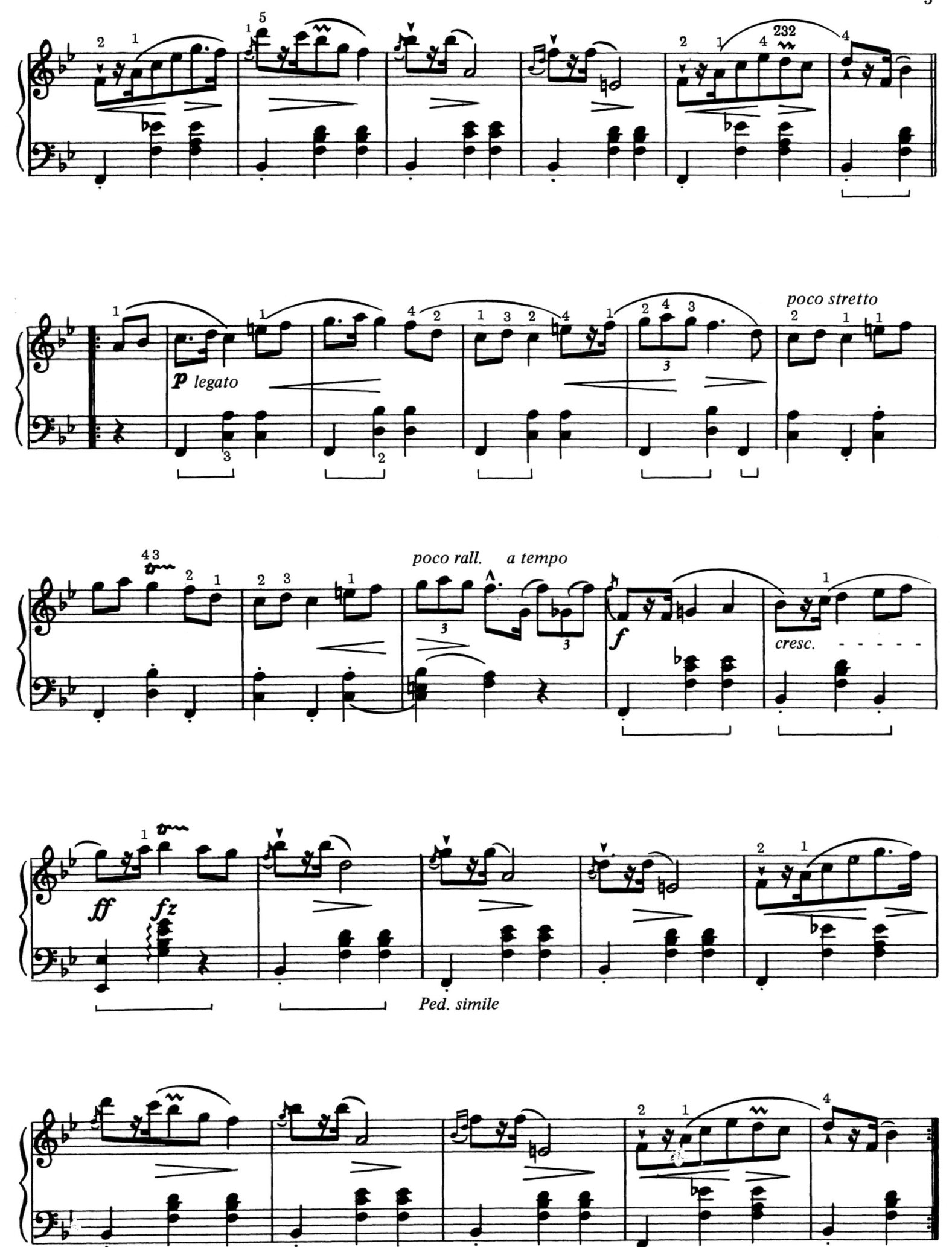

The minor mood of this mazurka is a deliberate contrast to the preceding selection. It nevertheless preserves the characteristics of the dance, but in a meditative style.

MAZURKA IN A MINOR

à Monsieur Johns de la Nouvelle-Orléans

Op. 7, No. 2

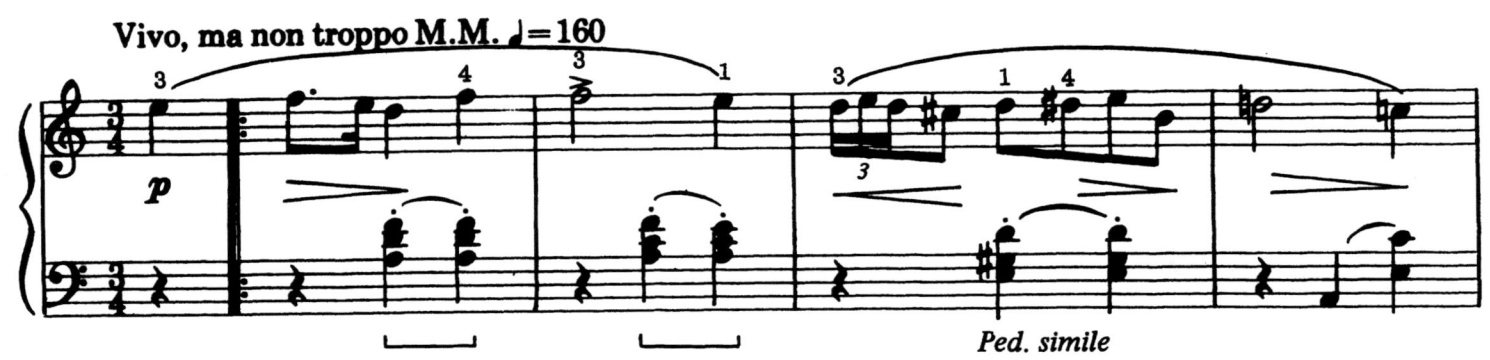

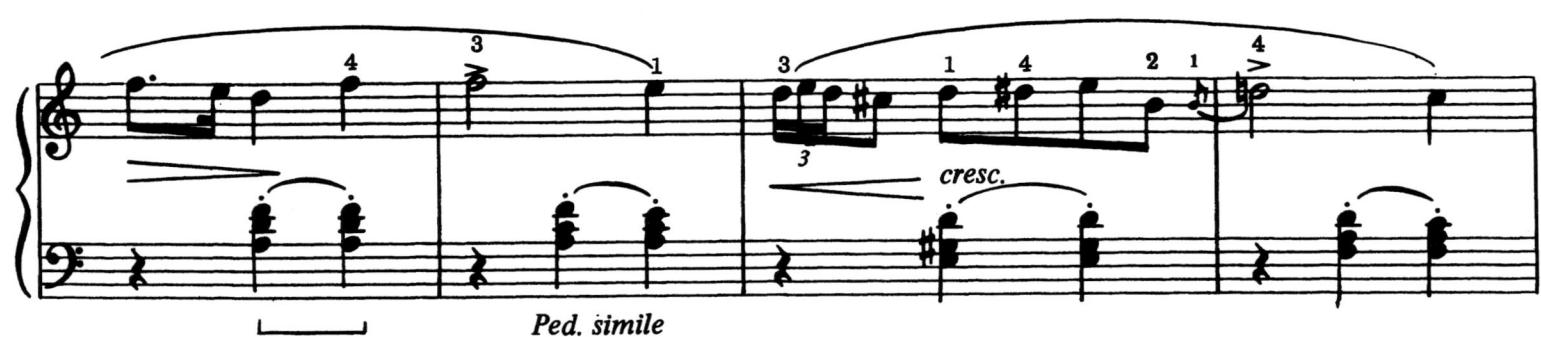
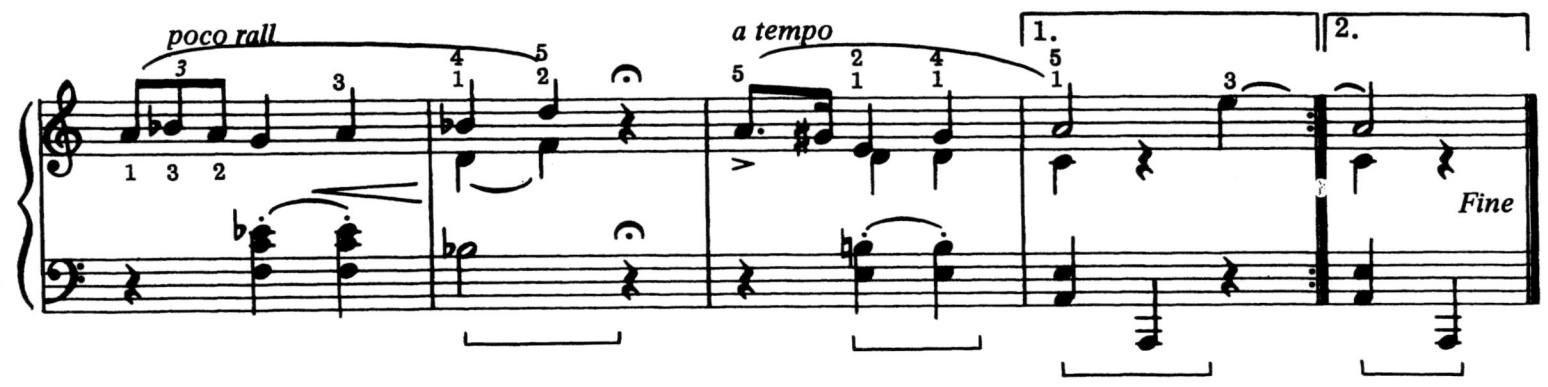

This very short mazurka is unusual in that it is marked *Dal segno* 𝄋 *senza Fine* (play from the sign 𝄋 , without ending). Thus the piece may be, in fact, a very long one, if you wish it to be. Repeat to the sign as many times as you like, and stop wherever you wish.

MAZURKA IN C MAJOR

Vivo. 𝅗𝅥. = 50-60 — *à Monsieur Johns de la Nouvelle-Orléans* — **Op. 7, No. 5**

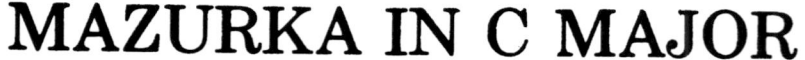

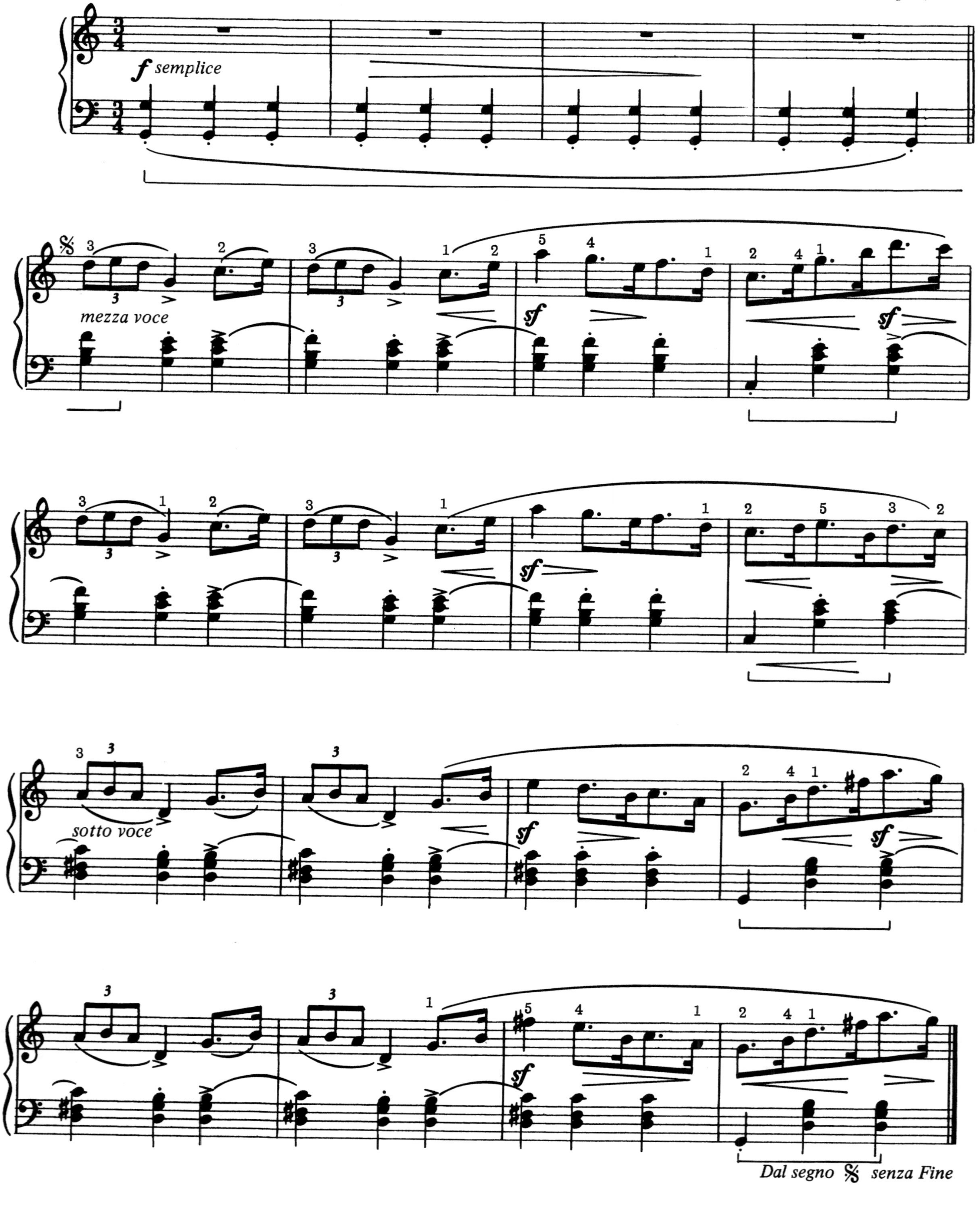

Although this is one of Chopin's shortest mazurkas, it is one of the most beautiful. According to Chopin's friend, Jules Fontana, who published his work shortly after Chopin's death, it was written in 1849, the last year of Chopin's life.

MAZURKA IN G MINOR

Op. 67, No. 2
Posthumous

During his own lifetime, none of Chopin's compositions enjoyed more popularity than his waltzes. It is a matter of record that no musicale was considered complete without a performance of at least one of his brilliant waltzes. The *Waltz in E Minor,* published shortly after his death, soon became one of the most popular. It combines the virtues of comparative simplicity with great brilliance, and is still a great favorite today, with students and concert artists alike.

WALTZ IN E MINOR

Posthumous

The beautiful opening melody of this waltz, played by the left hand, has made this an enduring favorite. Although it is one of the simplest waltzes, it is regularly featured on concert programs by the greatest artists.

WALTZ IN A MINOR

à Madame G. d'Ivry

Op. 34, No. 2

The *Waltz in Db Major,* has probably been performed more than any of Chopin's other compositions. It has been given the nickname, *The Minute Waltz,* with some disastrous results. Many performers have believed that the name indicated that the entire composition, including the repeated section, should be played in exactly one minute. Fortunately, this is untrue. Anyone who plays it in one minute is playing much too fast, and cannot possibly give the middle section the expressive treatment it requires.

WALTZ IN D♭ MAJOR

à Madame la Comtesse Delphine Potocka

Op. 64, No. 1

27

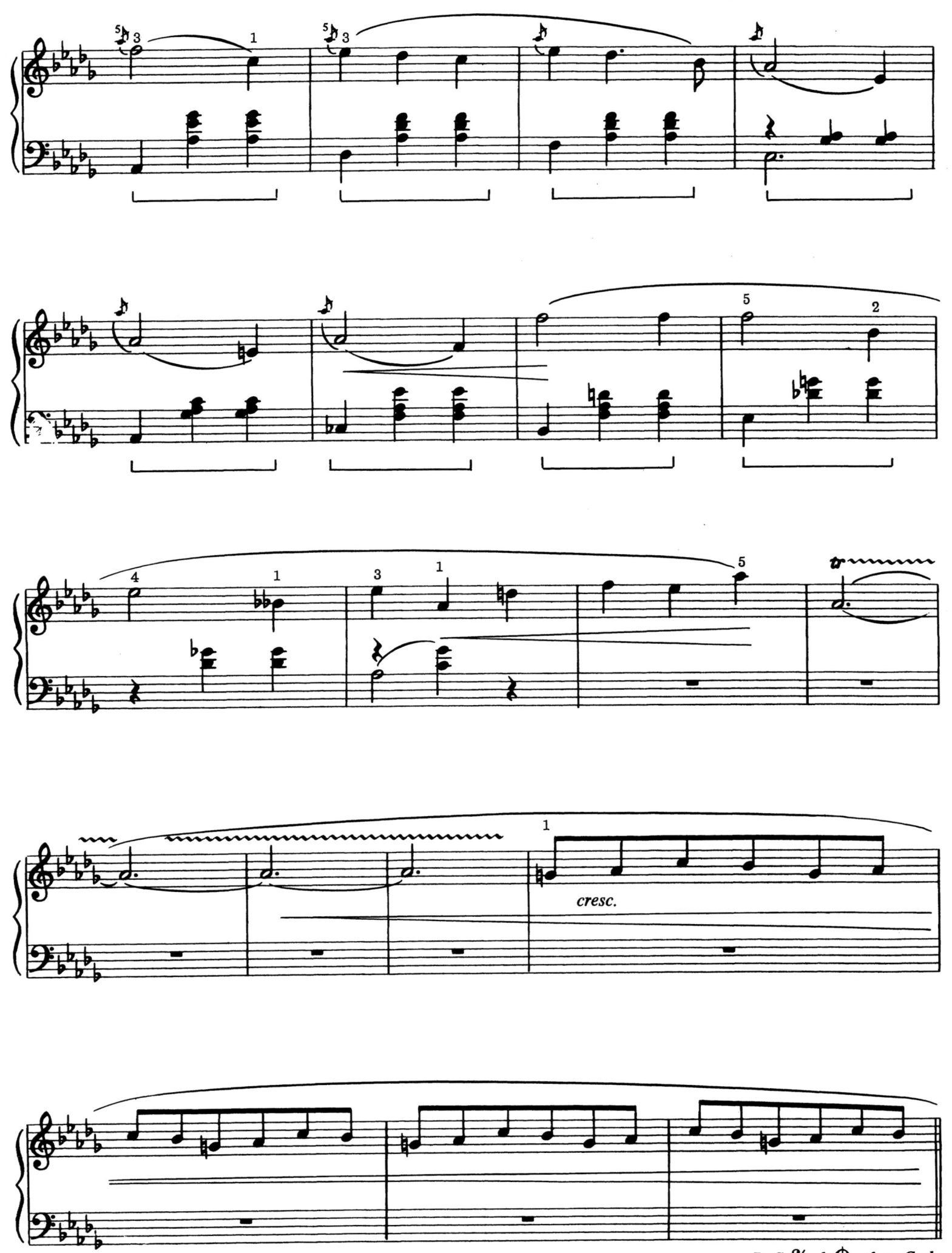

D. S. ⅌ al ⊕, then Coda

This waltz, the companion piece to *Opus 64, No. 1,* the famous *Minute Waltz,* is perhaps the second of the waltzes in universal popularity. The contrasting brilliance of the *più mosso* section with the lyricism of the opening melody gives it special charm and assures it a permanent place among the favorite works by Chopin.

WALTZ IN C♯ MINOR

à Madame la Baronne de Rothschild

Op. 64, No. 2

Tempo giusto M.M. ♩=116-126

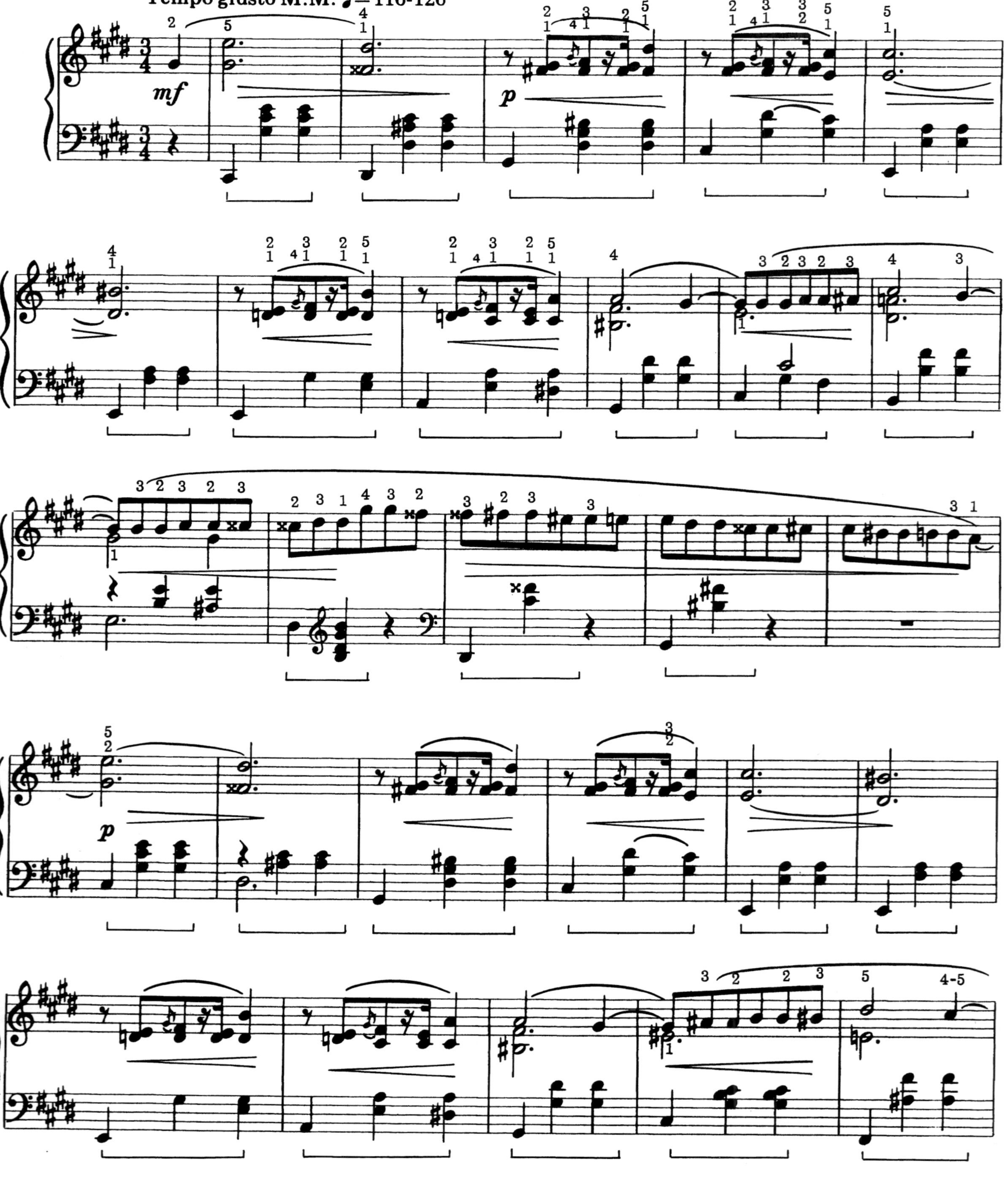

The *Twenty-Four Preludes, Opus 28,* were completed in the halls and rooms of an old monastery on the island of Majorca, in 1839. They were undoubtedly inspired by the preludes of J. S. Bach's *Well-Tempered Clavier,* which Chopin kept on his desk while he composed them. Robert Schumann considered the preludes to represent the very best of Chopin's compositions. On the following pages we present the best known of the *Preludes.* The 1st, in C Major, is certainly patterned after the 1st prelude of J. S. Bach, which is also in C Major, and uses a similar pattern of broken chord figurations.

PRELUDE IN C MAJOR

à son ami J. C. Kessler

Op. 28, No. 1

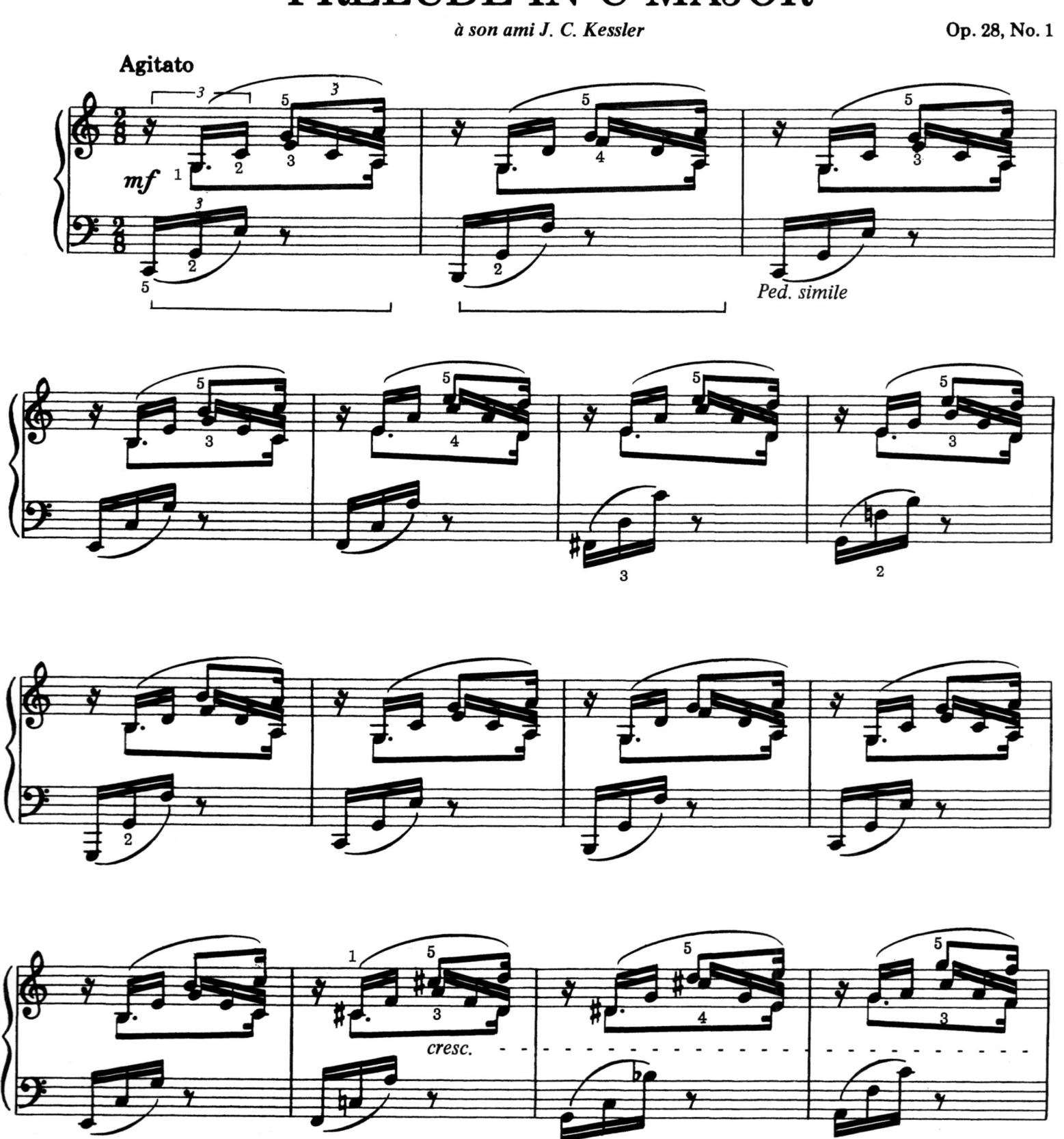

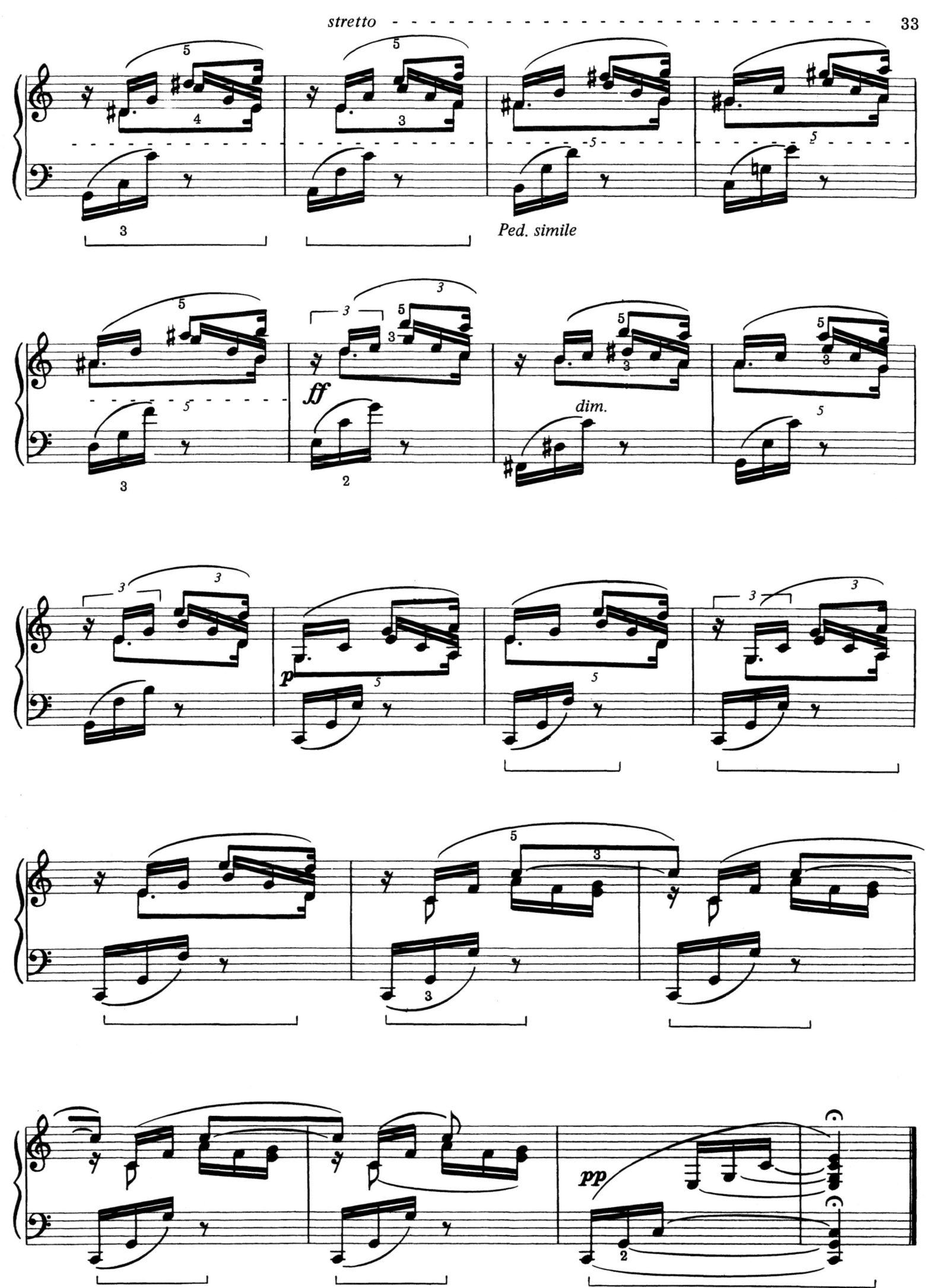

PRELUDE IN B MINOR

Op. 28, No. 6

PRELUDE IN A MAJOR

Op. 28, No. 7

PRELUDE IN E MINOR

Op. 28, No. 4

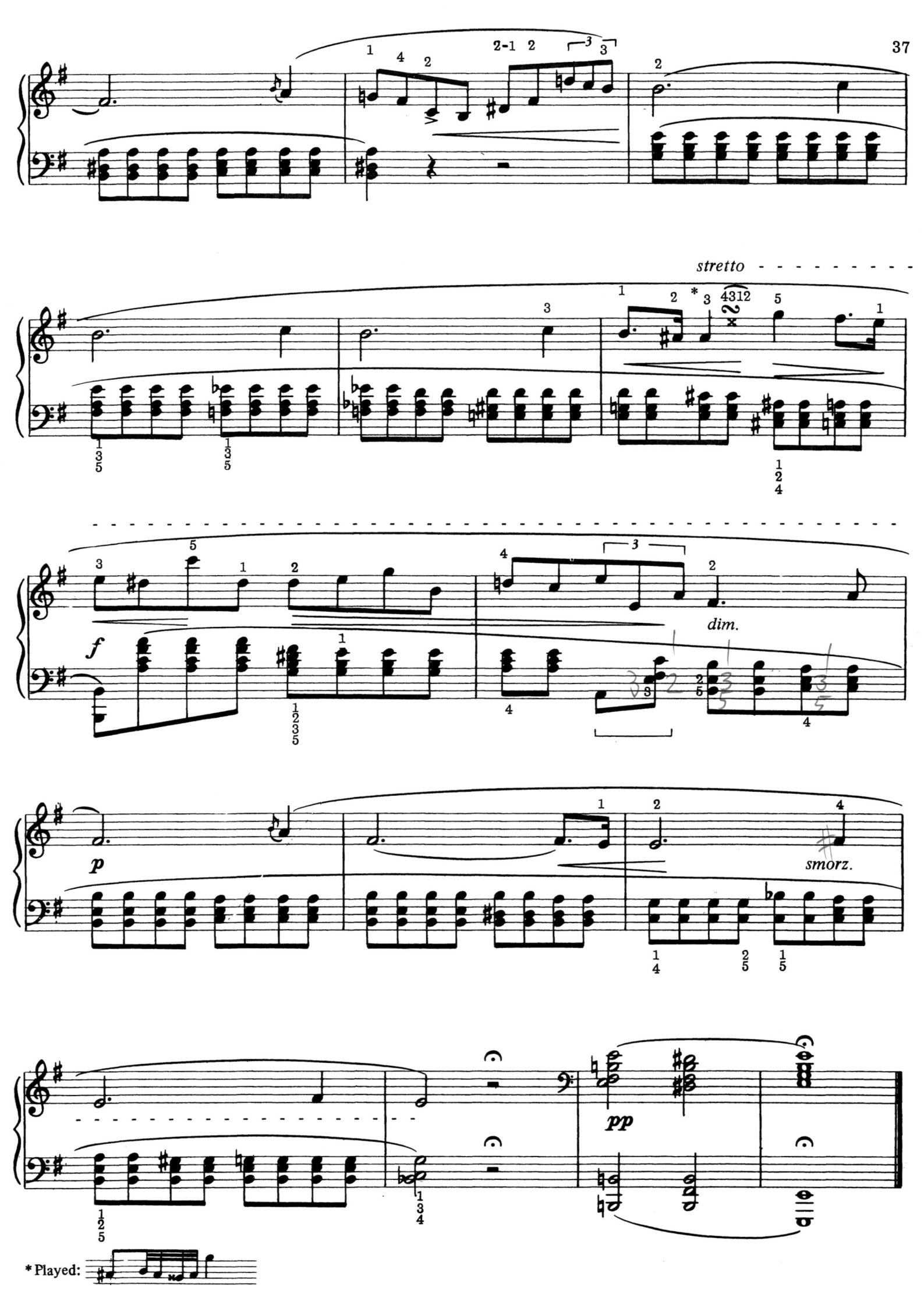

This is the famous *Raindrop Prelude*, so named because of the repeated notes in the *ostinato* that underlines the work from beginning to end. The middle section, in C sharp minor must have inspired the following words of George Sand: "Such vivid impressions are created in this music that the ghosts of departed monks seem to rise and pass before the listener in solemn and gloomy funereal pomp."

PRELUDE IN D♭ MAJOR

à son ami J. C. Kessler

Op. 28, No. 15

PRELUDE IN C MINOR

Op. 28, No. 20

This *Largo*, one of Chopin's most expressive short pieces, was only discovered in recent years. Play it very slowly and expressively throughout.

LARGO IN E♭ MAJOR

Posthumous

During Chopin's lifetime his nocturnes were second in popularity only to his waltzes. The *Nocturne in Eb Major, Opus 9, No. 2,* was then, and still remains, the most beloved of them all. Chopin inherited the form and basic style of his nocturnes from Clementi's pupil, John Field, whose beautiful touch and finished execution he greatly admired. Chopin greatly enriched the form and gave it dramatic breadth and beauty unsurpassed in music in this form before or after his era.

NOCTURNE IN E♭ MAJOR

à Madame Camilla Pleyel

Op. 9, No. 2

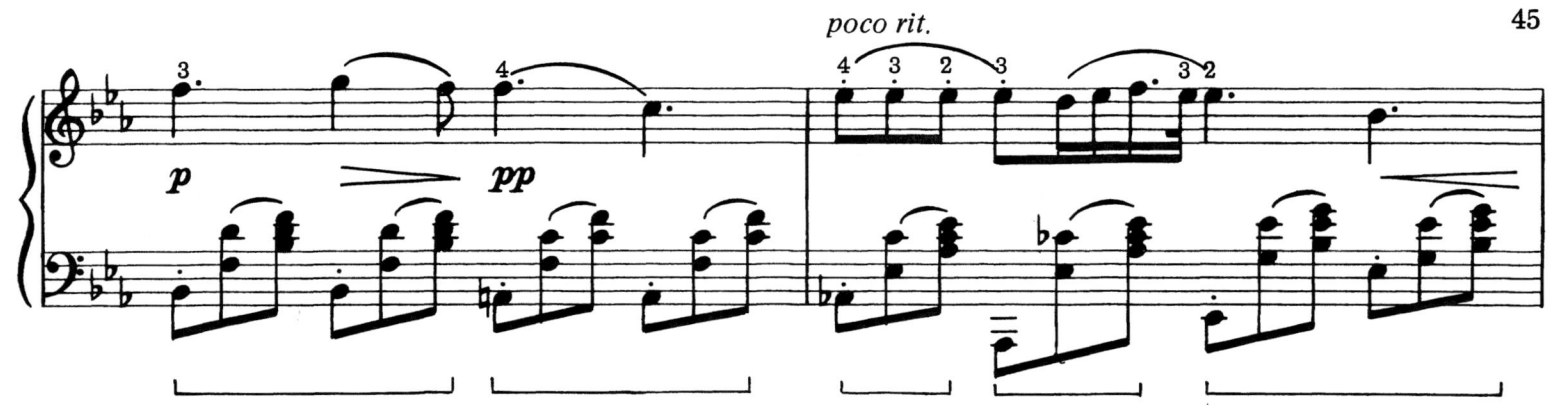
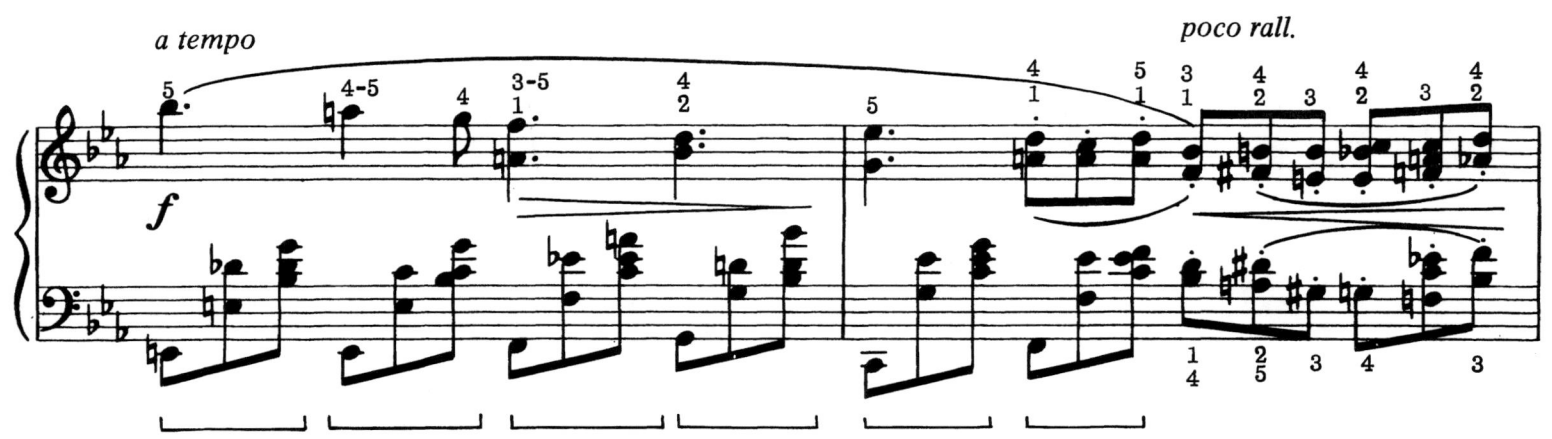
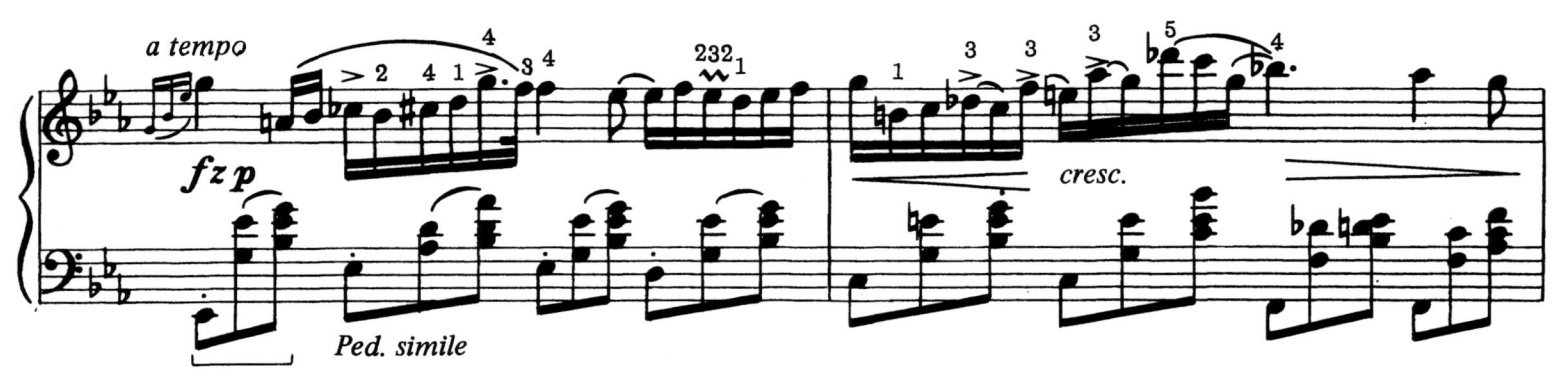

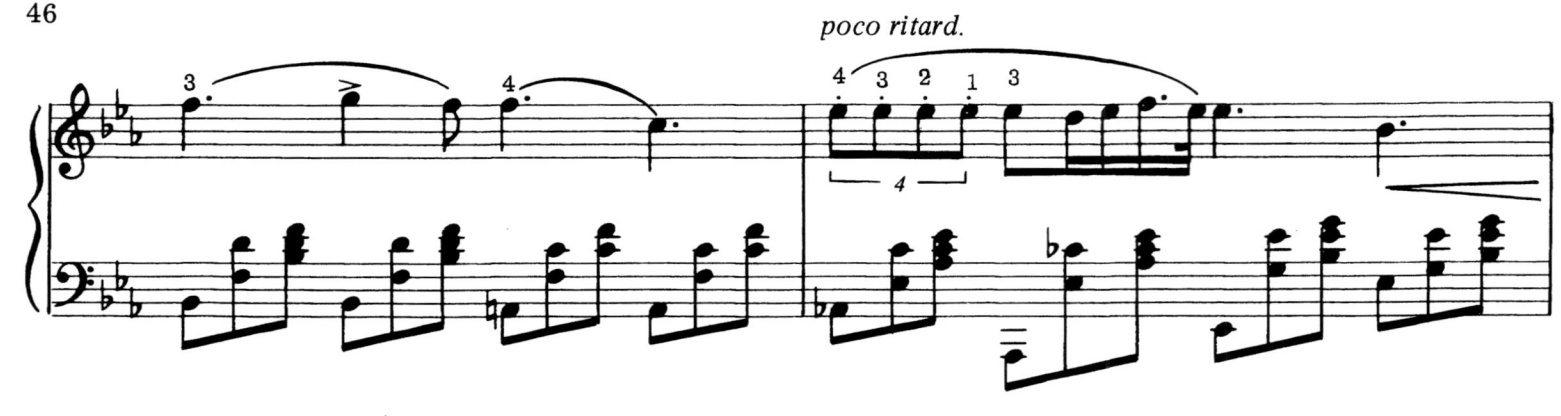

The polonaise is one of Poland's national dances. Before the time of Chopin the music that accompanied the polonaise was usually very simple in style and modest in length. In Chopin's hands the form assumed new proportions, and at the same time it became an expression of chivalry, pageantry and patriotism. The *Polonaise in A Major,* known as *The Military Polonaise,* was a sensation in Chopin's lifetime. Franz Liszt played it on nearly every one of his concerts. It still remains one of the most frequently performed works of Chopin.

POLONAISE IN A MAJOR

à Mr. J. Fontana

Op. 40, No. 1

The lyrical middle section of this composition has made it one of the best known works of Chopin. It has been simplified and rewritten in many forms. It has been made into a popular hit song. Here it appears as it was first published, only a few years after Chopin's death, by Jules Fontana, who was one of Chopin's closest friends.

FANTASIE - IMPROMPTU

Posthumous, Op. 66

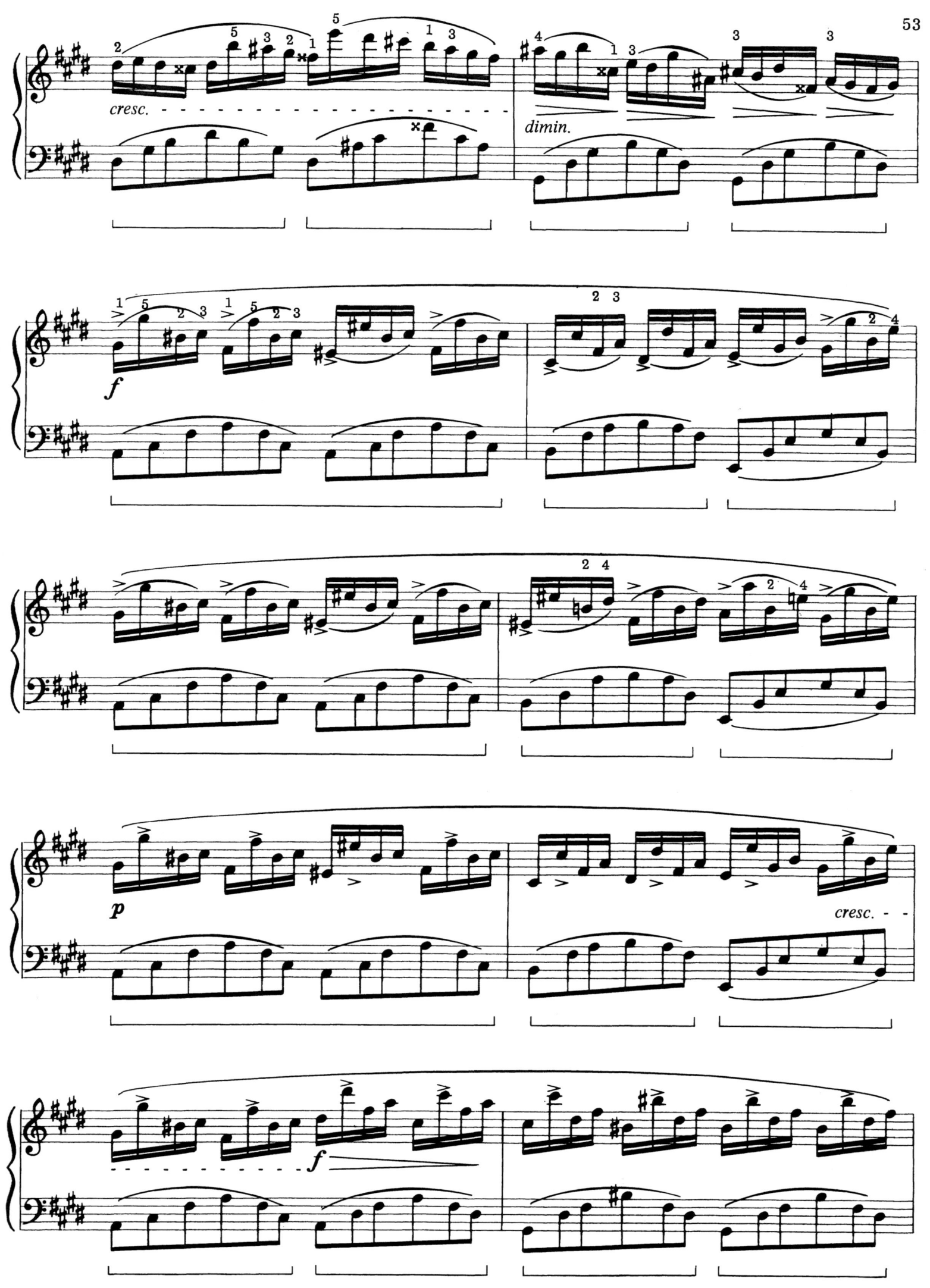

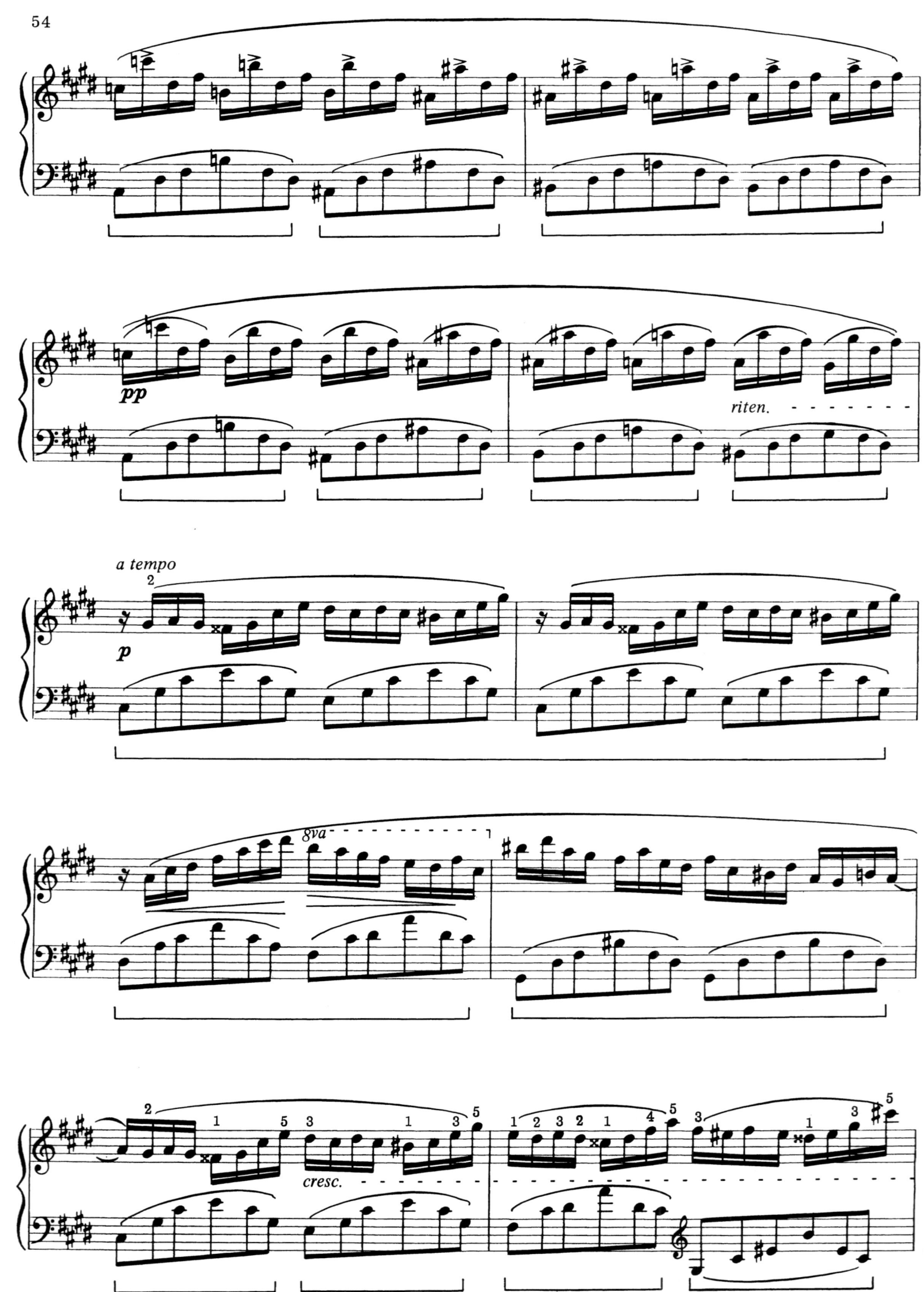

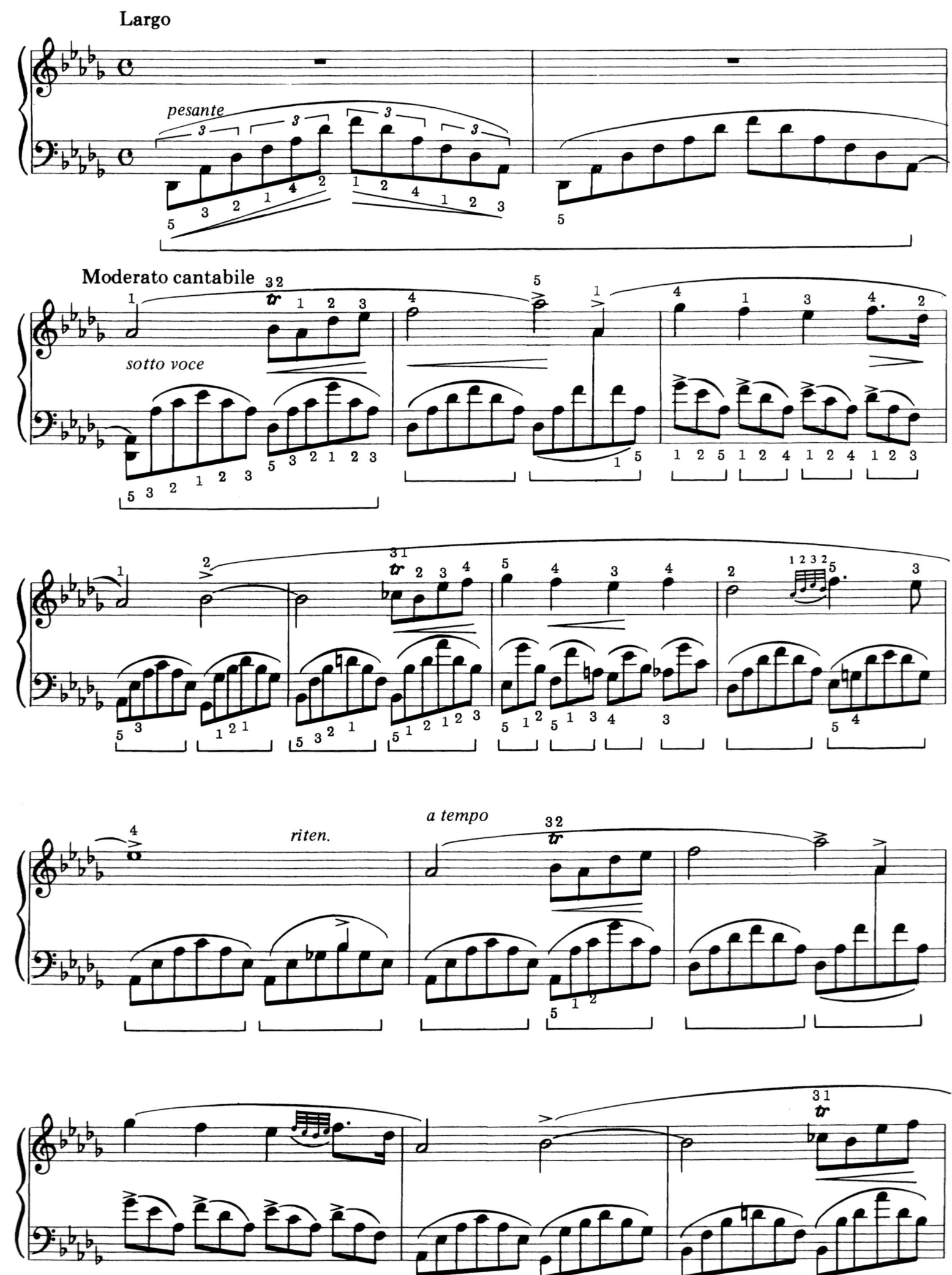

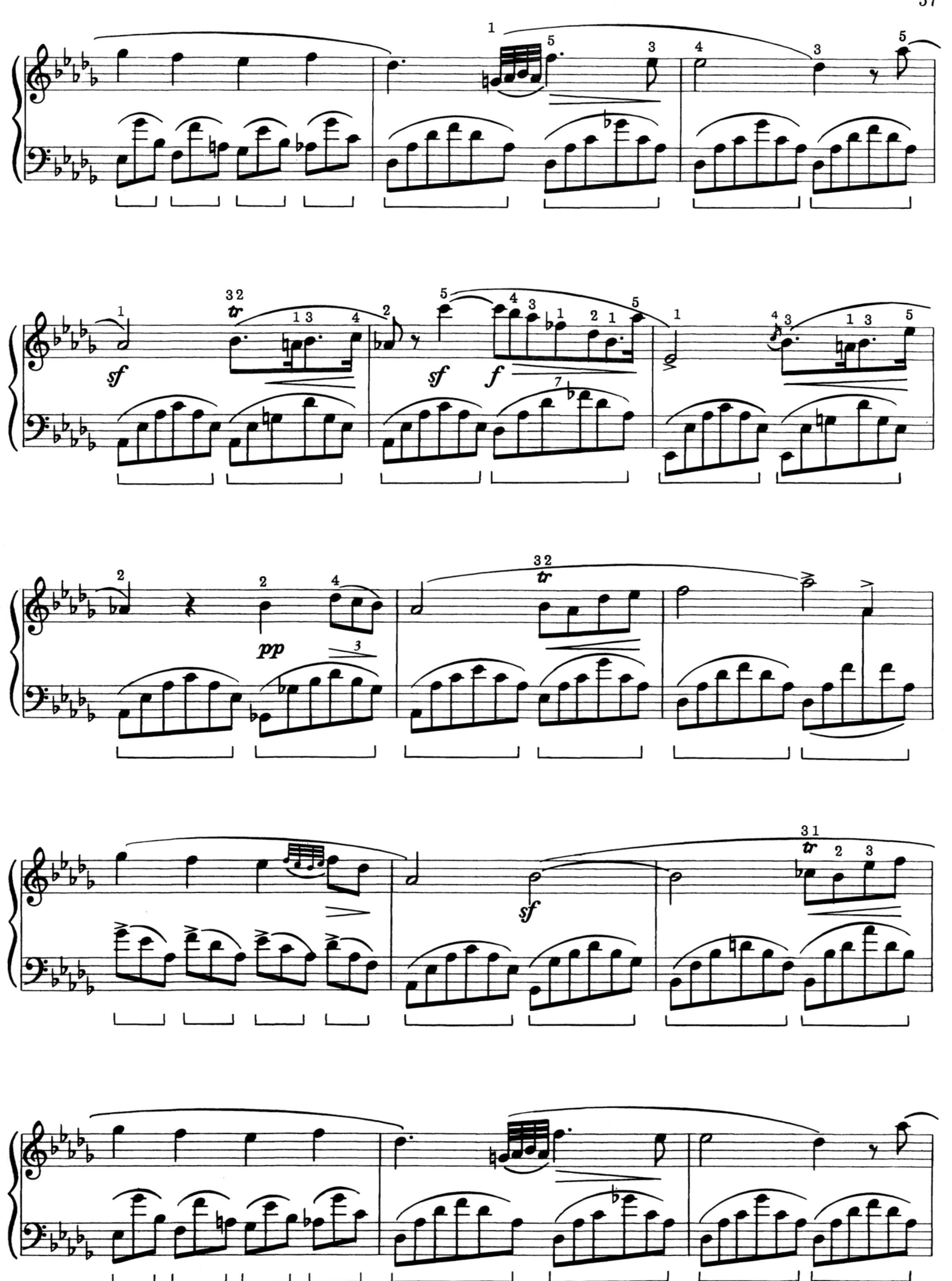

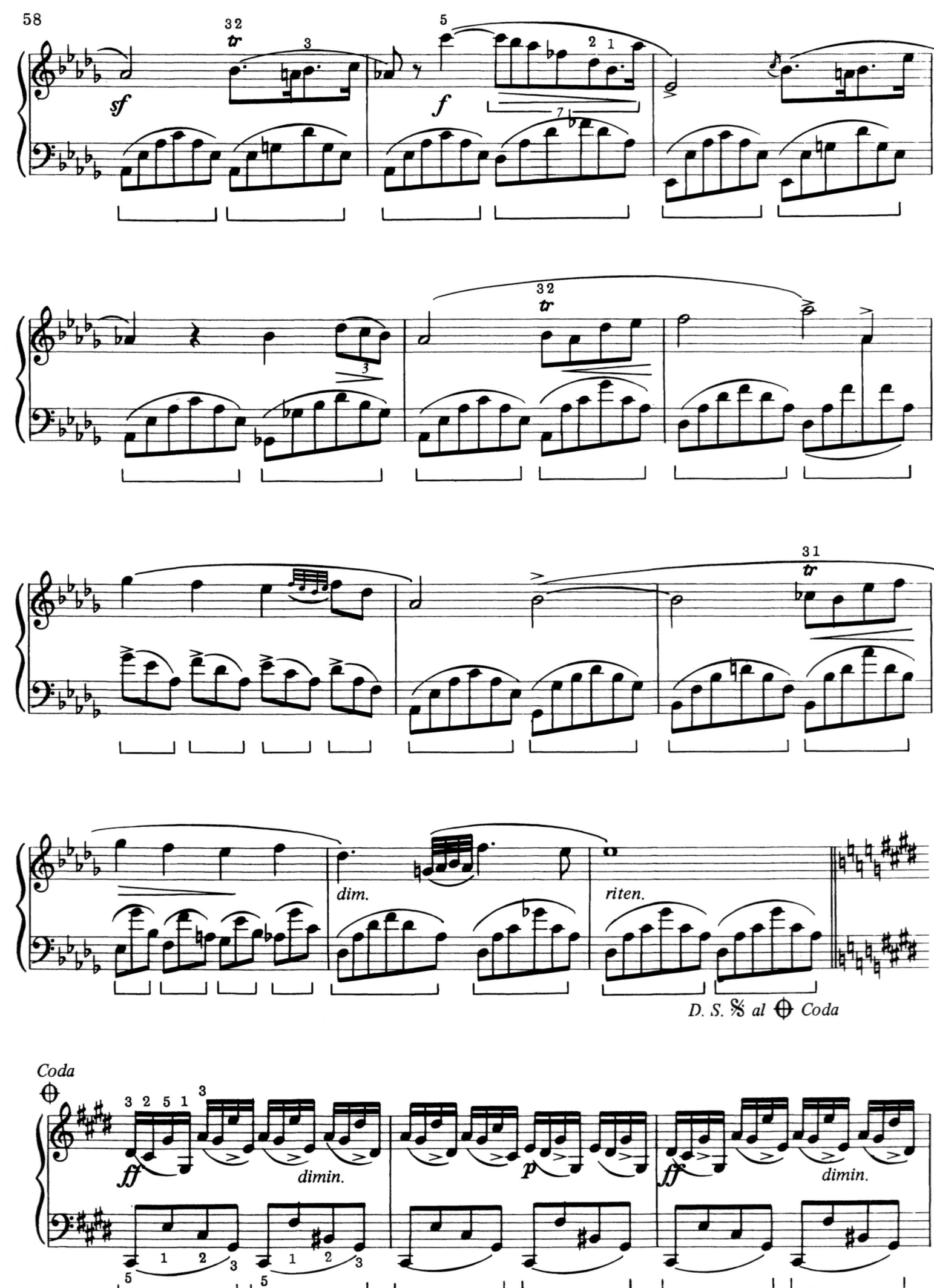

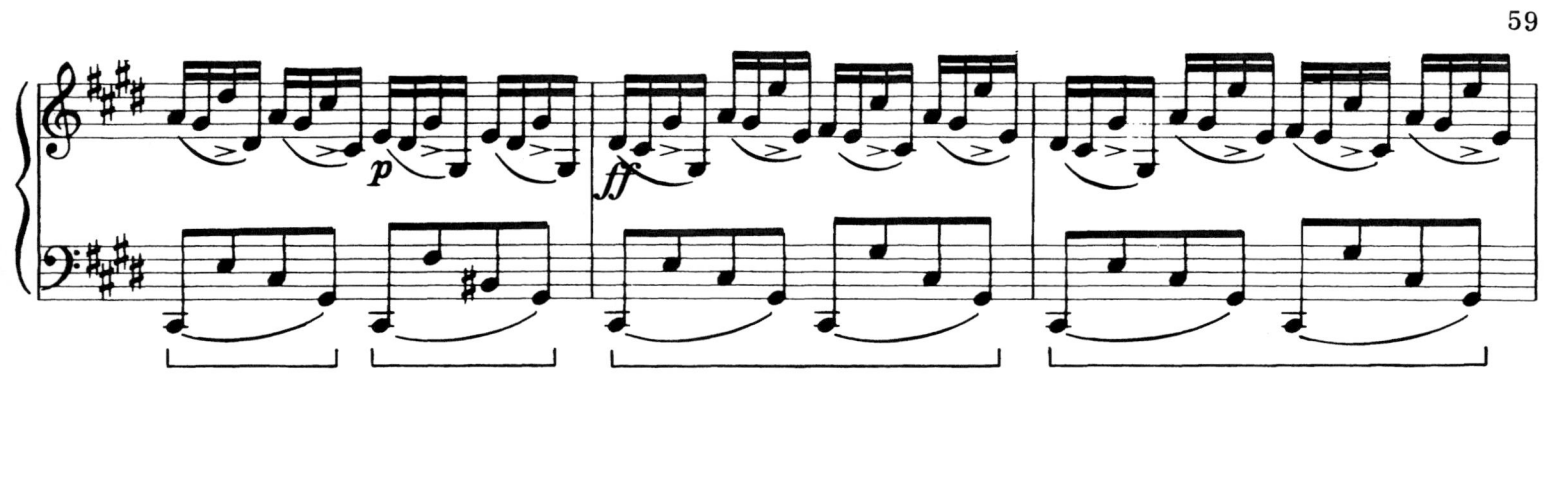

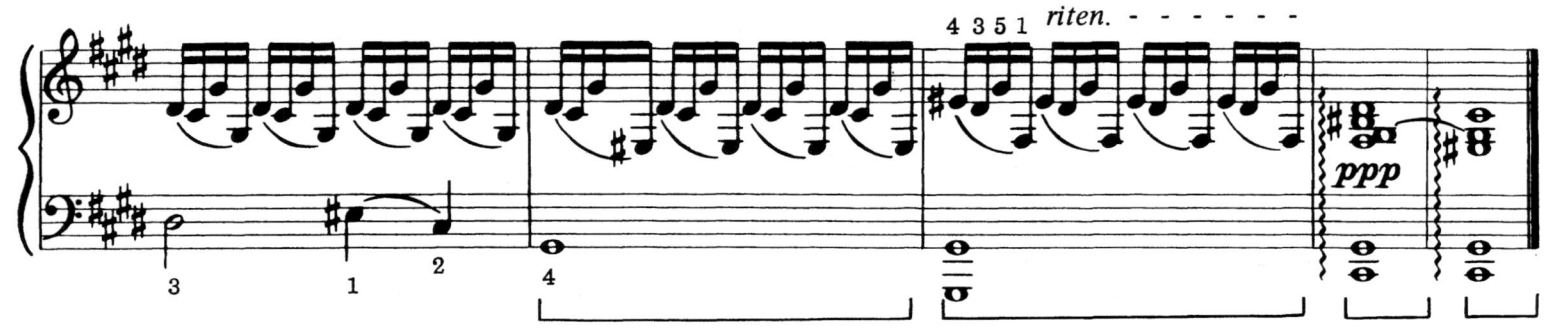

Of this piece, his most famous etude, Chopin said, "In all of my life I have never been able to find again so beautiful a melody." Many have agreed, and this work has been played in every sort of transscription. It has even enjoyed great popularity as a song. But no version has ever improved on the original form, which is faithfully presented here.

ETUDE IN E MAJOR

à son ami Franz Liszt

Op. 10, No. 3

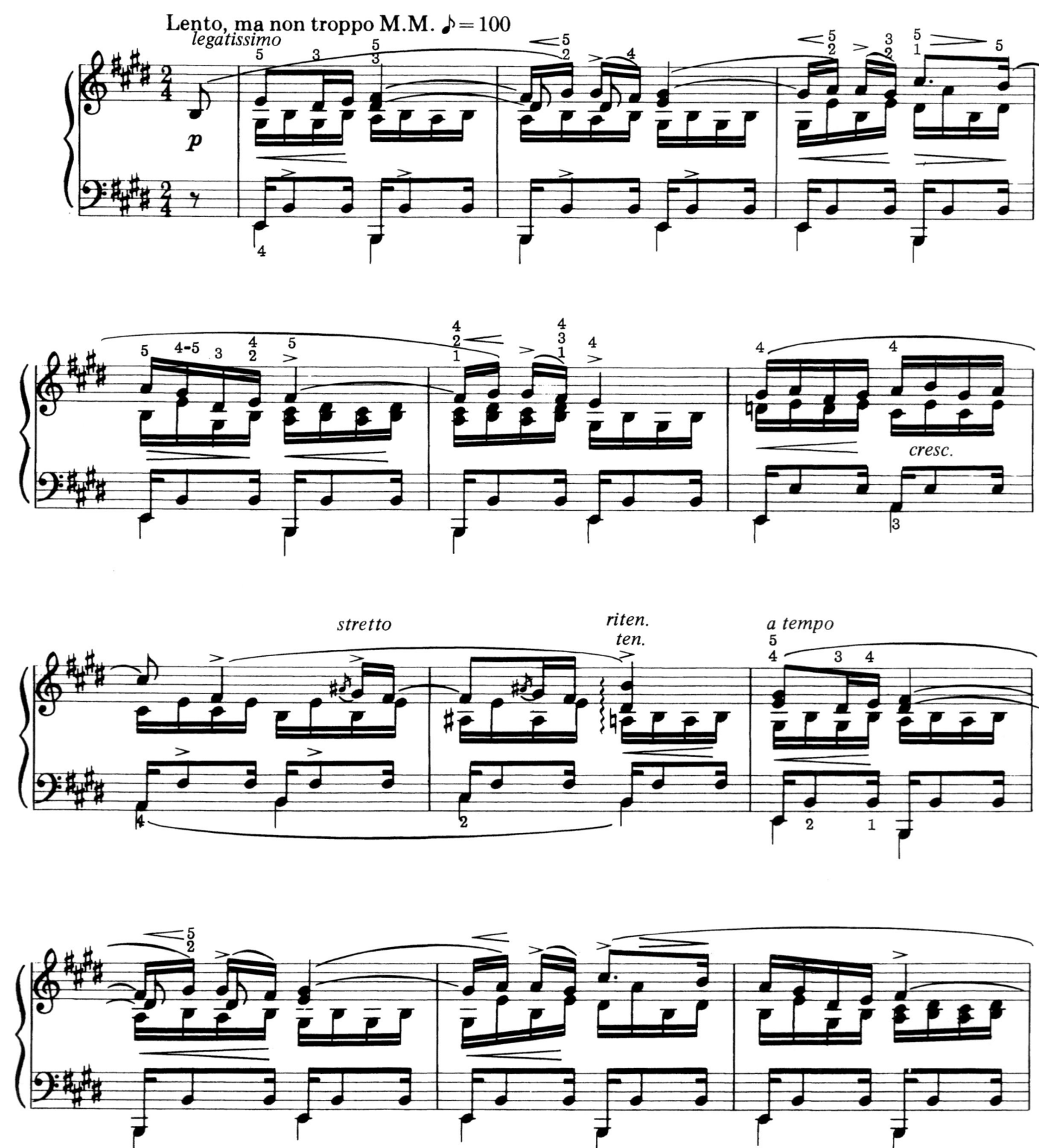

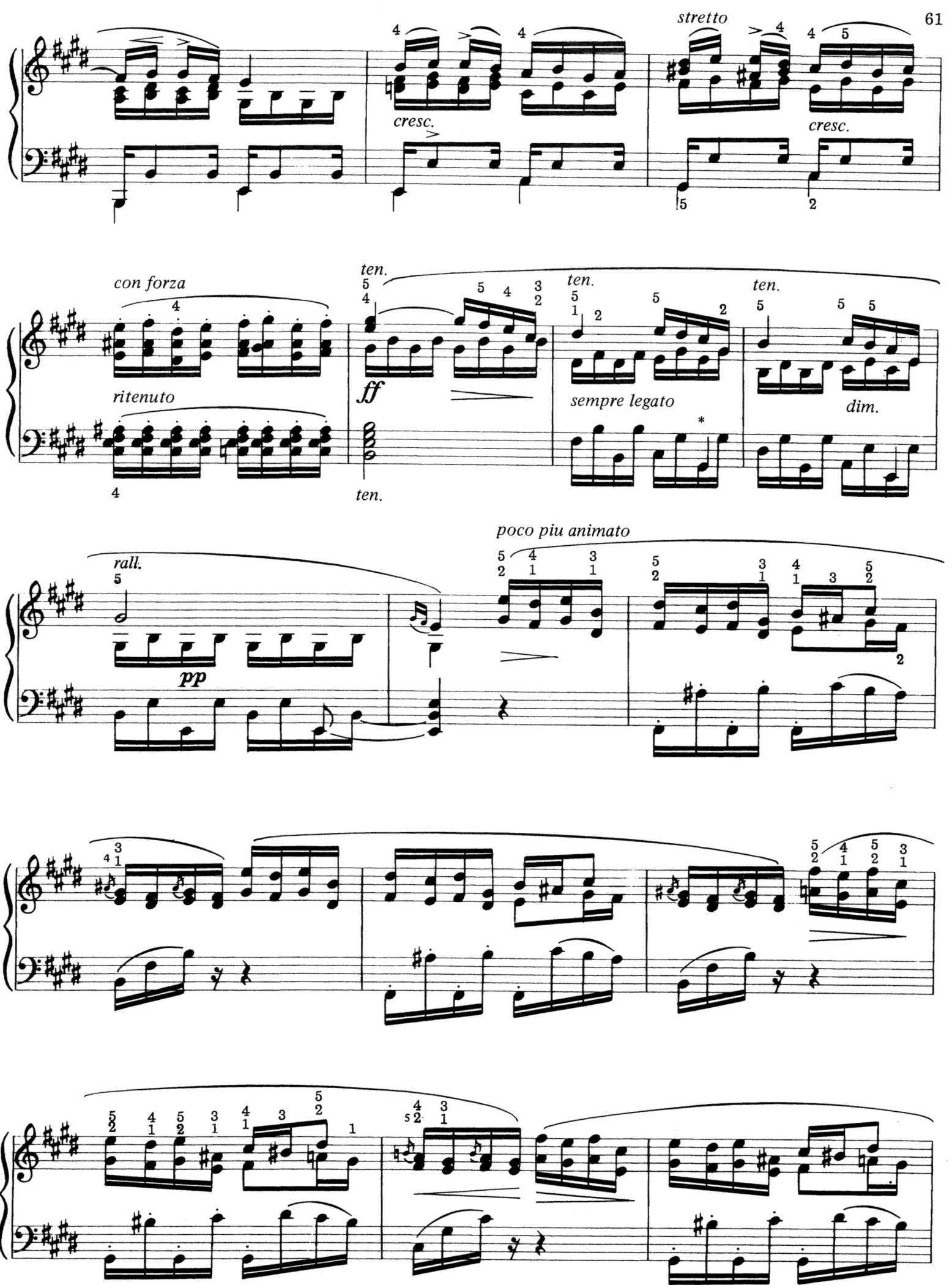

* The quarter notes with stems up in this and the following measures indicate the note is to be held into the following measure.